BOOK BENCHERS
PUBLICATIONS
PRESENTS

INSIDE EDGE

OF HEART

COMPILED BY -

MOHAMMED NIYAZ

YASMIN.S

AELAY PUBLICATION

A dream come true for every writers out there. We spot every possible problem for the writers, help in rectifying them and guide them towards the best outcome. We make sure to understand your needs, dreams and expectations, and nourish them with our services and stop not until we fulfill your dreams. The writers have a right and freedom to choose what they want here. They have us to guide them through the hardest path until the end. Believe in us.

Aelay Publication - by a writer for the writers.

BOOK BENCHERS

Book Benchers is the affiliate of Aelay publication. Both the publication is handled by Astro.
Aelay plays the role of publishing solo books.
And Book Benchers is epically for publishing anthologies.

Book Benchers have 2 different teams.
1. Tamil
2. English/Hindi

Never mind what our main motive is to help all the budding writers, who are seeking for their dream of publishing their own book to come true.

We are there to help out everyone.
In guiding for starting up with your carrier in compiling until finishing up your full book.

Book Benchers

COPYRIGHT

(Affiliate by Aelay Publish)

Book: INSIDE EDGE OF HEART
Compiler: MOHAMMED NIYAZ
Compiler: YASMIN.S
First Edition: Augest 2021

Published By:
The Book Benchers
5/175, Fathima nagar,
Kuthenkuly,
Tirunelveli -627104
Phone: 9944992571

Design And Executed by

ISBN : 978-93-5533-176-2
Page : 128

ACKNOWLEDGMENT

Alhamdulillah - With The Almighty's Grace!

If you have a heart, what's the most preferable chance you would take to read. Either reading yours or the others who keep on to holding the path of feelings. **"Inside Edge Of Heart"** under **Book Benchers Publication House** being compiled by **Mohammed Niyaz** And **Yasmin.S** respectively. We are thankful to the **founder Mr Astro Sir,** and the **Team Head Miss. KA. Parina Sri** for having immense faith in us to compile this beautiful anthology. We are also thankful to our **"51 co-authors"** for pouring out their wonderful thoughts under this book. We hope our readers have a great time out there with the same.

<u>DISCLAIMER</u>

"Inside Edge Of Heart" under **Book Benchers Publication House** is a work of fiction. All the thoughts, writings has been penned by the imaginative purpose of the writers itself. We do not take any responsibilities in case of plagiarism of content found as the publication, founders nor the compilers would be responsible for this. The writers will be the sole source of the above same.

<u>FOUNDER</u>

IRUDAGA ASTRO

Irudaga Astro, From Tirunelveli, Founder of
Aelay and BB (Book Benchers)
He had completed his BE.
He has written 3 Tamil poetry book's which
hits the top list on social media!
His main aim is to allow the writers to
publish their words as their book rather than
just Posting them on Insta.

LINK AND POSTER MAKER

CATHERINE ASMI T

Catherine Asmi T, From Tirunelveli
She has completed her M.com
Her passion is Drawing and Designing.

TEAM HEAD

She is a passionate writer from Chennai. Writing makes her pressure go away. She had played the role of co-author for more than 100+ Antho's. She would like to thank her parents and her Loveable Brother for supporting her rather than stopping her from what she wanted to do! For being the main reason for achieving her dreams. As well as for standing beside her in all the ups and downs. Whenever she feels like she needs to get out of her stressful timing or feels like she needs peacefulness, she starts to paint, she would never mind sitting in the same place for so many hours when it comes to her painting. She believes that anyone could hurt her, But never her books could!!

Catch her in Insta and FB
Insta: @theinnocentheart
FB: KA. PARINASRI

<u>INDEX</u>

27. ATHIRA.A
28. SRIJA SADHUKHAN
29. MANSI SOLANKI
30. BIBHUSMITA SINGH SAMANTA
31. ROZY PAUL
32. SRESTHA RAM
33. POETRY KHAKHOLIA
34. NILOFAR FAROOQUI TAUSEEF
35. MOHANAPRIYA.K
36. ANKITA NAHAR
37. GOURI VISHWANATH SALVI
38. SUMANDRITA PAUL
39. PRIYA DAS
40. RAVISHANKER NISHAD (ARVI)
41. SANA SHAIKH
42. KOVIDHA
43. S. T. RENUKA THANGAVEL
44. N. KRISHNAVENI
45. DEESHA SONI
46. V.S.KAARTHIKVEL
47. SHRIYA SINGH
48. UNNATI SAWANT
49. NAZRANA AHSAN WANI
50. PRAGATI GIRI
51. SRIJITA SAHA

MOHAMMED NIYAZ
(COMPILER)

मायानगरी मुंबई के रहने वाले मोहम्मद नियाज़ एक ड्रॉप-आउट इंजीनियरिंग स्टूडेंट है। शायरी की दुनिया में इनहोने अपना कदम साल २०१३ में रखा था। इनकी कई सारी शायरी फेसबुक और इंस्टाग्राम पर काफी मनोरंजीत करती है। यह भविष्य में एक राइटर बनना चाहते है। आप इनहे फेसबुक (Mohammed Niyaz) और इंस्टाग्राम (niyazsks) पर फॉलो कर सकते है।

दिल के कायदे

अदालत में आप की गुस्ताखी माफ़ है।
सुना है लगी आप पर ज़िम्मेदारी से कई अतराफ़ है।

यह कौन सा मोड़ ले लिया आपने के लौटना गवारा नहीं।
जहां रास्ते हो, मंज़िल कई फिर भी किनारा नहीं।

मगर फिर कसूर आपका आखिर क्या होगा।
इस तरह सज़ा को तोलने का अंजाम क्या होगा।

बस एक बार गहराईयों में उतर जाईयेगा।
कसम से खुद को पल दो पल की खातिर भूल जाईयेगा।

गर असर यह दवा आपके काम आये।
सुकून हो तब भी के कोई पैग़ाम नज़र आये।

यूँ कब तलाक अंधेरों में खुद को क़ैद करोगे।
राह-ए-उल्फत में बेखबर सब्र करोगे।

उम्मीद से अकल, एक तरफ़ा नक़ल कीजिए।
चौखट पे धड़कनों के मौका-ए-आस से निकल लीजिये।

दावा है मेरा, मंज़ूर-ए-मुनव्वर से मक़बूल है मेरे अक़ीदे।
खोज का एक ऐसा बसर, जिस में दिखे "दिल के कायदे"।

YASMIN.S
(COMPILER)

She is enlightened in Tamilnadu and proud to be a daughter.She has a Graceful and Sophisticated yet simple charm.She is an amiable.She completed her schooling at Sacred Heart Convent Anglo Indian Higher Secondary School and currently Accountant Student.She is a delighted Lassie.Her smile is infectious and she laughs all the time which everyone loves about her.When she started to taut a pen her hard days gave prime days.Though she's a challenger and much concentrated in her work to change life in prismatic.She is the QUEEN of his KING. She has executed 50+ Anthologies as a co-author and engaged with upcoming anthologies as a compiler And her favourite compiled books are which had been done with Niyaz and extricated to heave up with him and wish to continue forever.She is 19 years old.She is the One and Only YASMIN.

S.SUGANTHI

Suganthi has been writing for over two
years. She provides philosophical
writings. Her educational background in
English literature has given her a broad base
for writings. Her books are available in
Amazon Kindle named Heartly Sayings and
Healing journey-11

Instagram id - chum_moon

<u>WARRIOR</u>

When she needed
someone there for her.
No one stood by her side
She didn't lose herself
In the process of self-love
her aura resided.
When the toxicity made
Home to destroy her peace
Her aura choose to fight with cynical side
To set her from the anxiety
and traumatization.
every night come along with the darkness
You have to decide you wanna afraid
Or wanna be a warrior who fights.

MANISHA S KAUSHAL

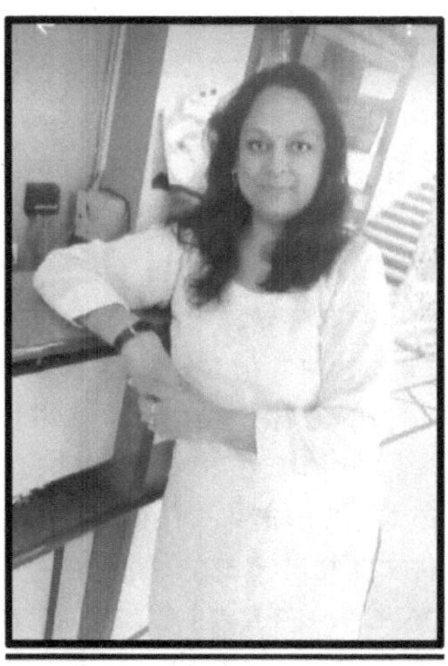

इनका नाम मनीषा कौशल है। झीलों की नगरी भोपाल की ये रहने वाली है। वर्तमान में ये श्री भवंस भारती पब्लिक स्कूल में हिंदी शिक्षिका के पद पर कार्यरत हैं। इन्हें लिखने का शौक बचपन से था परन्तु अपने शौक को कभी व्यक्त नहीं किया। कोरोना काल के अन्तर्गत मन में बसी हुई सारी बातें इन्होंने लेखन के द्वारा व्यक्त की। पिछले 15 वर्षों से ये बच्चों को हिंदी पढ़ाती आ रही है। लेखन क्षेत्र में ये और लिखना चाहती है।

Instagram id - Manisha Kaushal75

<u>दिल का रिश्ता</u>

दस वर्ष की मनु अपने सपने को लेकर बहुत परेशान रहती थी। उसकी समझ में नहीं आता था कि सपने में जो दिखाई देता है, वो कौन है? खैर उम्र के साथ मनु ने ये सोचा की ये सब कहानियों में ही होता है...असल जिंदगी में इस तरह कोई नहीं मिलता। "21" वर्ष की होते ही मनु की शादी हो गई तो उसे लगा कि अब सपना नहीं आयेगा पर ऐसा हुआ नहीं, सपना लगातार बना हुआ था। उस सपने के बारे में मनु ने किसी को नहीं बताया पर वो जानना जरूर चाहती थी कि ऐसा कौन है जो रोज़ आता है।दिन, महीने, साल बीत गए पर सपना नहीं बदला मनु ने भी सोचना छोड़ दिया था। तकनीकी क्षेत्र को लेकर फेसबुक काफी प्रचलित हुआ था, मनु ने भी सोचा की उसको भी उस से जुड़ना चाहिए। उसने भी अपना खाता बना लिया घरवालों के साथ - साथ अन्य लोगों के भी मित्रता के संदेश आए मनु ने स्वीकार किए। एक मित्रता का संदेश उसकी जिंदगी ही बदल गया। मनु ने उसे स्वीकार किया... हालांकि उम्र में काफी अंतर था फिर भी शुभ को और मनु को एक दूसरे से बात करना बहुत अच्छा लगता था। वो अपने कॉलेज की दिनचर्या और मनु अपने स्कूल की दिनचर्या की बारे करते थे। बहुत ही सुलझा हुआ रिश्ता...तीन साल तक सिर्फ संदेश से ही बात हुई, उसके बाद फोन नंबर एक दूसरे को दिए गए। इस बीच मनु को एहसास हुआ कि अब सपना नहीं आता। बहुत खुश भी थी और दुःखी भी। क्योंकि एक लंबे दूरी वाला रिश्ता जो निस्वार्थ सा था, वो उसको मिला भी तो कब?? और वो उसके पास भी नहीं रह सकती। यही सोचकर उसका मन विचलित हो उठा। उसने बहुत समय बाद शुभ को सपने के बारे में बताया और ये भी कहा कि अब वो सपना नहीं आता। पता नहीं दोनों के बीच ये दिल का रिश्ता किस तरह का है जो आज तक चल रहा है। मनु को लगा था कि शुभ की शादी के बाद ये रिश्ता नहीं रहेगा पर ऐसा नहीं हुआ, दूर होने पर भी, एक उम्र के ना होने पर भी, कोई लेन देन ना होने पर भी ये दिल का रिश्ता आज भी बना हुआ है और आगे भी रहेगा।

MADHUMITA

A conscious dreamer letting her thoughts out
through pen and paper

Instagram username - Feel.Free.Fun.24

Book Benchers

<u>DEAR BEST FRIEND....</u>

To whom we can irritate,
To whom we can fight,
To whom we can show some craziness,
To whom we can be angry,
The one whom we can say anything
Only you the one "Best friend"
To fix with you
Only we can call them with nickname
Only we can call them stupid to idiot
Only we can make each other to laugh
Only we make a bond to travel the world

Love you

LIPSA DABHI

She is lipsa dabhi. She is Author and also good Co-Author. She is eighteen years old, she is student of the computer engineering.She is extraordinary person. She is always good leader. Her mam mrunal prajapati is her inspiration person and also her motivator, her friend chetna raval also supported to her and her mom manisha ben and her father nilesh bhai also supported to her for anytype of her creativity.

she also wrote poems, short stories, shayaris.

Her writing skills almost very well and her creative collections are always best.

Instagram username - __lipsa__dabhi__0829

भाई तू अमूल्य

हर लम्हा आपके साथ बिताया वो बेमिसाल,
आपकी वो मस्ती और शरारते प्यारी हैं मुझे,
पलकों पर बिठाते आप मुझे हरदम,
मुझे मंजिल तक पहुंचने को सहारा दिया आपने,
हर ख्वाब को पूरा करना सिखाया ही आपने,
उठना बैठना आपके साथ हैं मेरा,
और आप से ही गहरा रिश्ता भी हैं,
शुक्रिया जान से भी ज्यादा प्यार करने के लिए,
संताकुकडी और हाँकी भी सिखाई आपने,
खुद मुझे बहुत ही परेशान करे आप,
पर किसी और की कोई मजाल नहीं,
बचपन का वो खजाना मुझे आज भी याद हैं,
वो खजाने का किंमती खजाना हो भाई आप,
भाई दुज ही नहीं हो कोई भी दिन,
आप रक्षा करते हो मेरी हर एक दिन,
मुझे सक्षम बनाया आपने और साथ दिया ।

रिंश्तो की डोर

रिंश्ते निभाना वो एक कला सी हैं,
सब रिंश्ते एक से नहीं होते,
कुछ अपने से और कुछ दिखावे के अपने हैं,
सभी रिंश्तो को वक्त दो आप,
हर रिंश्ते को समझो और पक्का रखो,
ना हार-जीत रखो कोई रिंश्ते में,
रिंश्ता कुछ बेहतरीन सी नींव होती हैं,
जो सज्ज होती हैं सहारे पर,
किसी तीसरे की वजह से ना टूटे रिंश्ता आपका,
भरोसा होना चाहिए हर एक रिंश्ते में,
भरोसे बिना ना मुमकिन कोई रिंश्ता,
रिंश्तो की डोर को पक्का रखना चाहिए,
एक प्यारा तोहफ़ा होता हैं रिंश्ता जिंदगी का,
रिंश्तो की बुनियाद ही बेहतरीन सी,
उसे बेहतरीन तरीके से समजाएँ हम,
रिंश्ता निभाना चाहिए हर किसी को,
वो ही होता हैं एक बेहतरीन नींव सा,
रिंश्ता कुछ अनमोल सख होता हैं ।

Book Benchers

<u>SONAL PRAJAPATI</u>

Instagram id - Misswriter_

<u>MY LIFE PARTNER</u>

In a world of full confusion
You are the one which is my compulsion
I carry all my desire
Because I want to be your fire
Having your hug in a day
It is like a shower in month of may
You carry my stuff all the time
Your every words matches words of mine
Your heart pumps thinking about me
Only this thing I can see, see, see
You are a true blessing to my life
I really really want to be your wife.

ANKITA SARKAR

Ankita Sarkar is a girl from Jamshedpur. She did her graduation on Hospitality Management and now majoring in Child Psychology. She has published her own book and has been a part of 7 Anthology books. She express her feelings through words.

Instagram id - ankitasarkar_4

<u>DARK THOUGHTS</u>

Those dark thoughts always hounds me,
Makes me feel depressed,
But that dark thoughts make me feel,
How courageous I'm,
To overcome from it.

ANKITA MISHRA

I am Ankita Mishra from Cuttack, Odisha. I am a student pursuing my graduation in bachelor's of commerce. Writing was never my passion nor my hobby. All I loved was singing, crafting and playing badminton. Then when I used to stay alone I used to write my feelings no matter happy or sad. And that's how I started writing by expressing my thoughts, feelings and emotions into words. I just hope and look forward towards taking this habit as my passion.

Instagram id - @the_imperfect_writer_08

<u>BEAUTIFUL</u>

Beautiful are those eyes,
that had cried for others in pain.

Beautiful are those lips,
that had prayed for everyone by name.

Beautiful are those ears,
that had heard every word spoken.

Beautiful are those hands,
that had picked up someone from trouble.

Beautiful are those arms,
that had consoled broken souls.

Beautiful are those feet,
that ran for someone in need.

Beautiful are those heart,
that had understood everyone's tough path.

<u>IMPORTANT</u>

Kids for their parents,
books for a student.

Pen is for a writer,
and patients for a doctor.

Plough for a farmer,
and brush for a painter.

Needle and thread for tailor,
a navigation map for sailor.

Music for a dancer,
and voice for a singer

Tricks for a magician,
and ideas for technician.

Importance about something
differs from person to person.

As nation's safety is for soldiers,
for a pilot it's his passengers.

SHASWAT SOURAV SAHOO

Shaswat Sourav Sahoo, is an eighteen-something adventurer who grew up traversing the wonders through the pages of metaphors. He fell in love with books and never reverted. Today he is pursuing his studies and living a clichéd life at NISER as an Integrated M.Sc. research scholar. He has been recently awarded with the Global Achievers Award.When he is not surrounded by words you can spot him fancying and pampering the dogs.He is a jovial kind of person revamping his past grief events into allured moments. He loves voicing his emotions and get it penned down.Another feather to his cap is his intense intimacy with taking shots. Nevertheless, he is also impassioned for painting, playing indoors, origami. He is looking forward his life being a polymath and pour on whatever he possesses within and wishes never to quell it.

Instagram id - __shaswat__19

<u>THE SWEETHEART</u>

Beauty at its peak,
Pure love that everyone seek,
Feed the emotions via her beak,
It's my mother to make me tweak.

Her soul is divine,
Her care is upto the cloud nine,
She is the one who holds thee,
Beyond this cruel world up so fine.

HAR DEEPANSH BAHADUR SINHA

He is Har Deepansh Bahadur Sinha .
He belongs to Lucknow,UP.
He has done masters in Geography from National
Post Graduate College.
Completed his schooling from Study Hall.
His hobbies are art , listening to music , cooking &
loads of driving.
His interest areas are Astronomy, Writing,
Photography & Travelling a lot.

Instagram id - Deepansh_sinha

<u>YOUTH NEEDS TO BE SUSTAINED</u>

Youth is the important part of society
But they are degrading their own identity,
They are not taking things practically
Towards life they are approaching casually.

Living in the sunshine but walking towards dark
They are losing their inner spark,
Without attaining any experience they think they are
expert
Everyday every second they are getting divert.

For them it's necessary to come out from Illusion
With elders they need some serious discussions,
They must know their priorities
Along with that their responsibilities.

They have to put aside their aggression
Must think twice before taking actions,
Gathering public and bringing boys is senseless
Rise above all these things are useless.

PRACHI GUPTA

Prachi Gupta is a Passionate writer who loves to create her imaginary arts in a random canvas. She is pursuing her studies in BBA and lives in Allahabad known as The pure city of Sangam.

She loves to sing and watching movies in her free time.
She is a shy and a open-minded girl at the same time

For more information can follow her and contact:-
Prachiguptt0210@gmail.com

@prachigupta3435
@prachi_gupta_210

<u>NEVER</u>

Never say, "No"
If you don't feel too

Never say, "Yes"
If you don't feel to

Never "apologize"
If you don't feel to

Never "sympathize"
If you don't feel to

Never "involve"
If anyone don't want to

Never "speak"
If anyone don't want to

Never "let it go"
If you don't want to

Never "Do"
If you don't feel to

Never "forget"
What you want to do...

ANANYA P MISHRA

Myself Ananya P Mishra from Bhubaneswar, Odisha. I'm a student of English Honors. Believes in karma. Bookaholic. Want to set an example for this era that inspires others and me as well. Love dancing, designing and exploring new things. Self-love is priority. Always know your worth.

Instagram id - ananya_payal191

<u>MADE FOR EACH OTHER -</u>

She was unable to remain
cold and distant,
when he was crumbling before her
she kissed him back,
her breath hiccuping softly over his lips
and then she slipped her palm
across the slid bristle of his jaw
dropping his cheek in a simple gesture
of acceptance and understanding,
Of forgiveness.
They forgave each other
And made love like never before.

ABHISHEK SINGH PARCHA

अभिषेक सिंह पर्चा ये 12वीं पास है और ये स्टेनोग्राफी विद्यार्थी हैं

इन्हें लिखना बेहद पसंद है, ये दिल्ली के कमल पार्क में रहते हैं ये रैपर लिरिक्स और कविता करते हैं । इन्हें लिखने की प्रेरणा डॉ. राहत इंदौरी साहब से मिली है

Instagram id - Abhishek_singh_parcha

आज दिल किया चलो उसके लिए
कुछ लिखा देते है
अब तो मोहब्बत करना गवारा लगता है
चलो आज फिर मोहब्बत कर लेते है

#अभिषेक
(अभिषेक सिंह पर्चा)

आसमान में बादल छा रहे हैं
बारिश होने तेरा नाम लिख दिया
नाम तुम्हारा संध्या है
मैंने उसे बड़े प्यार से अभिषेक कर दिया

#अभिषेक
(अभिषेक सिंह पर्चा)

अकेले में बैठकर रो रही हो लगता
है
तुम्हारा दिल टूटा है
और तुम करती थी उससे सच्चा प्यार
लगता है वो तुम्हारे जिस्म से प्यार करता है

GAJAL TAYAL

Gajal is a girl of her own world with a lot of dreams in her eyes. She is a medical student and soon became doctor. She love to write and want to explore world. She is a coauthor in 110+books and compiler of book "love and pandemic "

Instagram id - @gajal27

<u>दिल से निकली बातें</u>

जब दिल से कोई दुआ निकलती है
तो वह जरूर मुकम्मल होती है

तुमने सोचा
तेरे दूर जाने से भूल जाएंगे हम
पर तुझे भुला ना इतना आसान नहीं

मजबूरी तो सबकी होती है
पर जो प्यार करते हैं
वह निभाते जरूर है

तुम साथ हो मेरे
मेरे लिए यही काफी है
बंगला गाड़ी का शोक मैं भी रखती हूं
पर इतनी कामयाब हो जाऊंगी मैं
इतना यकीन है मुझे खुद पर

HARSHITA VERMA

Co-author Harshita Verma is a writer from Lucknow. She has completed her graduation in commerce stream. She has been writing poetry for the last few years as her passion. She wants to be a novelist in future.

Instagram id - 0___hsh

<u>DREAMS</u>

The dreams inspiring to achieve great things
The dreams not allowing to sleep in nights
Dreams inspiring and motivating to achieve the
unexpected
These dreams are different not to be forgotten even
when awake
Everytime bringing new courage when remembered
Achievements a result of our hard work inspired by
the dreams
Everytime there is a motivation in life to achieve the
goals
The parameters inspiring to reach them as soon as
possible
The life full of hurdles but the motivation are the
dreams
Inspiring to follow the path of our choice and be
successful
Whatever happens in life the dreams are to be
fulfilled
The inspiring modes of our life never forgotten

PAYAL KAMDI

पायल कामडी महाराष्ट्र की रहने वाली है | इंद्रधनुष्य की तरह साथ रंगो से दिलो की कहाणी जोडकर अतूट का रिश्ते बना लेती है | अपने विचारो को नित्यश्री उपनाम से कलमबध्द करती है | दिल और दिमाग से खिलवाड करके लिखने की लगन वाली लडकी, स्याही उठाकर कागज के नीचे गिर गयी जो छाया के बनकर उसके साथ आती है | वह विश्वास करती है की लेखन ठोस विचारो को ओर तेजी से प्रकट होने मे मदत करते है | अपने प्रेम के प्रति उसे विश्वास है जो साथ ना रेहकर भी उसे प्रोथसाहन प्रदान करता है और जिणे की आशा देता है |

जब प्रेम नहीं आता हाथो की लकिरो मैं
तब प्रेम से अधिक सर्वश्रेष्ठ का प्रसंग आता है
उसे केहते हैं मान सन्मान

मैं नहीं करुंगा तूम्से वादा
ना गुलाब का, ना चांद का
बस वादा करता हू
हर पल साथ देणे का

एक जीवन मैंने खुद की पैचान मैं गवया
लोगो ने मेरी पैचान पुचकर
उस्से मुझे ही हरा दिया
मेरी पैचान मेरे समाज से जुडा दिया

मैंने एक पल के लिये देखा
मेरा दिल हर पल उसके लिये धडका
एक ही दिल है
वो भी तुम्हारा हो गया

ANUSHA SATHIA

Anusha is a writer and a poet hailing from India. She is currently in high school. She has been writing since quite a few years and that has been her passion. She uses her positive attitude and tireless energy to encourage others to work hard and succeed and she writes because she enjoys expressing herself. For more of her work, please check out her Instagram handle: @_thelittletherapist

Book Benchers

I know broken is beautiful
for I have seen the breaking of dawn.
I know burying something doesn't mean the end of
it
for I have seen plants bloom from seeds buried
underneath.
I know happiness awaits people who feel hurt
for I have seen mothers cry during labor and the
smile that follows afterwards.
I know I don't know a lot of things
but this much I know to be true,
time and tide may wait for none
but good things wait for you.

DHARSHINI.M

She is dharshini from kovilpatti. She is pursing masters in English. She has huge interest in writing.she loves to share her thought and emotion through her writing.She has done many anthologies as co author . She has published a book named 'vox of mine '.

Instagram id - dharshji_dharsh

<u>QUOTES</u>

Life rush us to take decisions
Mind says do things which make all happy
Hearts says do things which make you happy

Sometimes we have to choose one
Without thinking it's hurts all
If we give importance to all
You will loss your happiness

The problem in choosing their dream
Is the guilt that it may hurt their parents
And end up in losing it
For the sake of them

The pain of sacrifice is huge than oceans
In that tears place a role more
Where love stands still in heart

People who believe in them
Are mostly unbelieved by all once
For sure will became believable soon

Make things better
By leaving the negativity
And be on the path of positivity.

RAJESHWARI PANDIAN

Once, A Princess named RAJI PANDIAN surfed in
the sea of love,
Then a vasty wave sinked her;
And made her to lost her way;
Then she found a lighthouse which drives her in the
correct way- INKING.

Instagram id - Raji pandian (Dreamer_24_ji)

<u>MOVING ON</u>

Why the silence of someone affect her the most¿
Is there any statute ?
As love only has the power to missing?
Nah!!!
There is real love in all kinda relationships,
Don't wipe someone's tears if you're not ready to
continue it,
Don't train them for longing for your company !
If moving on is easy for you,
Don't except that quality in others!
If the little changes in you affects her greatly,
Then realize the amount of love she had for you!

DAKSHITA JAISWAL

Dakshita jaiswal is a 18 year old Management student. She is from Gonda, Uttarpradesh. Being a voracious reader and writer, She has organized multiple events and itself is a poet, storyteller, blogger and a published author.
She is the core team member of Happy hearts organization, an event organizing house. She inculcates high interest into the field of writing and have performed at various platforms. You can search her on Instagram @invoicer_dakshita_jaiswal.

<u>CAN I BE MY LAST HOPE ?</u>

Yesterday, My hope cried for Eight hours,
Wrecked with emotions, My Believe went dark,
Dark in the slimmer silver lining of clouds, bursting
with Pain of doubts,
Doubt that awakens me from my Dream of shroud,
Breaths couldn't reside my heart,
Eyes were frozen with Arch's,
Swelled up throat, dead mouth to erode,
Blooded limps, with a mark of Failure,
Failure that could deceive My Faith,
Could one nerve can shut their Says?
Bearing the unbearable pain,
My heartbeats were leaving my soul in vain,
Bewildered by shiva's Plan,
Drenched with Betrayal, Disrupted to trust His Idol,
My mind was clogged,
In the dim light that agogs, across my faith and my
trusts,
Challenging my esteem to build upon a thrust,
Thrust which holds the gesture to fight,
A thrust which could Enlight,
My fear would be my last shroud until shiva's
delight,
Reckoned to hear, but enough of tears,
Love to rebel and hate to deny,
Filch destiny, Let's conquer and fly high,

Let's cease the story,
Through revenge of Glory,
Of countless cries, I pledge to fly,
Can I be my last hope?
Hope that smiles with divine eternity,
Promises to learn, live and love,
with Eccentricity,
To be my labour of love,
Hope with an oath of Desire,
An inevitable end of arousing fire.

ANKUR MISHRA

बातें अपनी दिल की इस कदर किया करते हैं,
जज़बात को बयां कोरे पन्ने मे किया करते हैं।

ये हैं अंकुर मिश्रा जो वर्तमान मे देवास मध्यप्रदेश मे कार्यरत एक उभरते हुए लेखक हैं जो कि जिंदगी और नौकरी का संतुलन बनाये रखते हुए अपने लेखन के शौक को जिंदा रखे हुए हैं। इनकी रचनाये पच्चीस से ज्यादा ई-बुक/किताबो मे प्रकाशित हो चुकी या होने वाली हैं। भविष्य मे ये अपनी सभी रचनाओ को खुद की पुस्तक मे संजोने का ख्वाब रखते हैं। इंस्टाग्राम मे आप इनसे अपने विचार ankdip2801 मे साझा कर सकते हैं ।

वक्त

माना आज हताश हो तुम,
इतने जो निराश हो तुम,
दुनियादारी का अजब खेल है,
मतलबी मनो के गजब मेल है,
जरूरत है जगाना जमीर को,
तोड़ डालो भ्रम भरी ज़ंजीर को,
तुम अकेले खुशी के गरीब नही,
हमेशा रह सकते खुशनसीब नही,
रखना मत हर वक्त खामोशी,
रखो अपने अक्स से सरफरोशी
सबको हासिल होता ये दौर,
समझ लो ये बातें करके गौर,
कभी कभी नसीब से जाती है उमंग,
पर नही रहेंगे कभी हमेशा ये बेरंग,
कभी वो बेवक्त भी इस कदर आता है,
जब वक्त भी दर-बदर सा हो जाता है ।

चलो सुबह मे हो मलंग

नया सवेरा नयी उमंग,
पंक्षियों की धुन दबंग,
सूरज को छुपाये मतंग,
अरमानो की उड़ी पतंग,
मन मे उमड़ी मौज तरंग,
लेके हौसलो को अपने संग,
जीतकर उठो सुस्ती की जंग,
भले करे नींद कितना भी तंग,
न कर पाये ये ध्यान भंग,
बिखेर के फिर मस्ती के रंग,
मायूसी से करके मोहभंग,
लोग सब देखे हो जाये दंग,
ऐसा उत्साही हो अपना प्रसंग,
छोड़ के चादर और पलंग,
ताजगी मे डूबा के सब अंग,
चलो इस सुबह मे हों मलंग ।

PRAKASH TURIYA (RAGHUWANSHI)

Prakash turiya, from chhindwara, madhya pradesh, M.pharma. working as senior executive medical writer

Instagram id - light@Raghuwanshi

<u>कुछ तो बाकी सा है.....</u>

कुछ ख्वाहिशे ही सही, कुछ फर्माहिसे ही सही।
कुछ तो बाकी सा हैं, जिंदगी में कही।।

कुछ अल्फ़ाज़ तो कहे, कुछ रुक से गये।
कुछ तो बाकी सा हैं, लफ्जो में कही।।

कुछ सपने बुने, कुछ अपने बने।
कुछ तो बाकी सा हैं, निंदो में कही।।

POETESS MANISHA KAMARAJ

She is Manisha Kamaraj pursuing Computer Science Engineering in KSK college of engineering and technology. She lives in Ammachathiram, Tamilnadu. Even though her future career is Software Developer, but she feels proud and satisfied for being a poetess. She has capability of writing poem and quotes in both Tamil and English. She currently works at her father's shop as Managing Director. She was a co-author for 30+ anthologies. She was a Computer Science tutor in urbanpro. Follow her in instagram @manisha_furniture_mart.

<u>NO CHANGES ; ONLY CHANGES</u>

In my life journey,
Many situations, I had crossed,
Many persons, I had met,
Many moments, I had spent,
There is no change,
In the above events...
Routinely, I had problems,
Because of my attitude,
Because of fake peoples,
Because of irritable memories,
There is no change,
In the above events...
There is an change,
In my mindset,
That I need to work hard,
Than before...

PRAKHAR RAGHUWANSHI

I am Prakhar Raghuwanshi from betul city of madhya pradesh and I am 15 years old currently studying in class 12th. I have been involved in the field of writing specially in poetry since last one year.

Instagram id - prkhrrghuwnshi_1

"अस्थिरता"

अस्थिर अब सब कुछ हुआ है,
स्थिरता की अब तलाश है।
संशय सा सब कुछ हुआ है,
आश्रय की अब आस है।
अब विडम्बना कुछ ऐसी आई,
कि अस्थिरता स्थिरता सी छाई।
अनेक विचारो का कम्पन लिए,
विचलित सोच मन में समाई।
अब इन जटिल विकारो से,
विचार विमर्श करना है मुझे।
जूझकर इन सभी विचारो से,
निरंतर आगे बढ़ना है मुझे।
ऐ ईश्वर मुझे साहस दे,
अब मुश्किलो से लड़ना है मुझे।

NAVEEN BHARDWAJ

Myself Naveen bhardwaj a programmer by profession a lover of poetry maker and like reading books and audiobooks and he has telegram channel @TheNBbook
insta I'd na.vin7832

There are millions of people in this planet and we care about the person who says no to us how cruel. We should start our journey again instead of thinking for someone who doesn't bother about our feeling. Sometimes we give importance to people who doesn't care about our love , compassion and feeling .

We all busy in doing something , we all human being don't have time the problem is we give more importance to thing which doesn't work for us and ignoring the things which is best for us . It's a worst feeling ever when other tries to explain us the importance of role in their life.

We all born in this world with some deformity yet we feel that we are not enough . Why these question develop in our mind. Instead of thinking about what we don't have let's start experiencing new challenges in our life . Practice mindfulness And meditation say thank to god what we have.

PRIYA SINGH

Priya Singh is born & brought up in Dewas,
MadhyaPradesh.She's a Proud daughter of her Father
B.N.Singh (T.I.). She's completed Masters of Computer
Science.She is a Former Educationist, Communication Trainer
& Avid Reader.
She's the Co-Author of the Anthologies:-
"It's all about two phase : love & hate" ,"Words From Heart",
"Fierce, Fearless N Flawed" & "In the way of borehole",
"Unseen Blessings & "Sublime Love", "Mere Papa".
All are available in Amazon.
Till today, She's worked in 230+ Anthologies as a Co-Author
& compiling 3.
Her writing keeps her at ease.
She mostly write quotes on thoughts.
She loves inspiring young minds.

Instagram id - instant__thoughts_

<u>MOON TRAVERSES</u>

The moon travels
everywhere,
it sees me but
I stay still &
See you in moon,
It lets me pander
dealing with the music
that life croons,
Wishing you had
loads of things to
come back to your
place now
&
hoping to see you
soon.
****

<u>MESMERISING THOUGHTS</u>

Even when I close
my eyes,
It let me dies,
Your every single gaze,
made me hassle
&
fly upto highs,
Even when I deny,
I get sigh with every gaze
of yours
&
always try to
get one more time
heed as phase.

KALAMKAAR

इनका नाम कलमकार है ये उत्तराखंड के रहने वाले है , मगर मेरठ में रह रहे हैं ! इनको लिखना और पढ़ना पसंद है! इन्होने 870+ अन्थोलॉजी में सेह लेखक के रूप में काम किया है और 750+ सम्मान पत्र जीते है! इनको लिखना और पड़ना पसंद है!इनकी रूचि लिखने में है!इनको कर्म पर विश्वास है फल से ज्यादा! इन्होने 20+पुस्तक में भाग लिया है सह लेखक के रूप में जो रिकॉर्ड के लिए गयी है!

Instagram id - Kalamkaar51

<u>तुक्का एक बार लगता है हर बार नहीं</u>

मेहनत करते है जीतने के लिये हर प्रतिभागी!
गिरके उठते है फिरसे मानते वो हार नहीं!
बना लेते हो बाते तुम बढ़ी आसानी से किसी की काबिलियत पे
सवाल उठाकर!
मगर याद रखना तुक्का एक बार लगता है हर बार नहीं!
दिमाग़ का खेल होता है सब जीतने के लिये हर परिस्पर्धा!
हारता वो ही है जो कोशिश करता जीतने की लगातार नहीं!
तुमको सिर्फ हार दिखती है जीत जाये अगर फिर बाते बनाते
हो तुम लोग!
जीत हाज़िल करने के लिये मेहनत करनी पड़ती है क्योकि
तुक्का एक बार लगता है हर बार नहीं!
ऊँगली उठना बहुत आसान है किसी के चरित्र पर!
जो झेला उसने उस जीत को पाने के लिये समझो उसको
क्योकि तुम्हारी समझ से है वो बाहर नहीं!
मत उठाओ ऊँगली किसी पर जीता अगर वो तो शाबाशी दो!
क्योकि तुक्का एक बार लगता है हर बारा नहीं!
मानो अपनी गलती जो हुई तुमसे अकड़ मत दिखाओ किसी
को!
मानोगे नहीं गलती अकड़ दिखाओगे तो हो तुम समझदार नहीं!
जीत के लिये ऐड़ी चोटी का ज़ोर लगया है उसने!
क्योकि उसको भी पता है तुक्का एक बार लगता है हर बार
नहीं!

ATHIRA.A

Co-author Athira. A is a young poetess from Ernakulam, Kerala State. She has completed her Bachelors in Science stream from St. Teresa's College, Ernakulam. She has been writing poems for 15 years as her passion.Athira is the compiler of poetry anthology 'Camaraderie'.Book reading and reviewing is also her major hobby.

Email :- athiraorminnu@gmail.com

Instagram id - _athira_a_

HEART OR MIND

I am left alone here
In utter dilemma;
Constantly thinking
Whether to listen to
The words of heart,
Or the silence of mind.

At times heart speaks,
Pouring out the words
Like a roar of waves;
Induces in me an urge
To speak out all those
Hidden secrets of mine.

But, soon the heart is
Won over by the mind;
And this dumb mind
Drags me into Ocean
Of profound silence,
With words left untold.

A HYMN TO GOD

Oh, dear God, here i am,
Standing in front of you,
With hands folded and
Lips filled with prayers.

It may seem annoying,
If i ask you to give ears
To each and every wish
That i am praying for.

You have indeed filled
The life of this pauper,
Always with showers
of abundant blessings.

Oh, dear God, here i am,
Standing in front of you,
Trying to find apt words
To sing to you a hymn.

SRIJA SADHUKHAN

Srija Sadhukhan is 19 years old girl studying BSc Biotechnology in Amity University Kolkata. Love to write poetry and a book worm too.

Instagram username - Syncopatemysuccess

GET OXYGEN FREE

Passing by, she is lost in the lore of trees
The Boughs, twigs and odd gnarled
Branches holding each other tightly
To breathe free, stop cutting trees.
The most precious gift God has given to us is nature
She sings earthen melodies from soul
But where are the trees?
To breathe free melt away the hatred of weapon
For cutting down the trees
Create a shield against humans to protect
environment
She saw the green land turns into barren land,
The peace she use to enjoy under the shadows of the
leaves
And the happiness of life from sun kissed rays
But now she want to stop deforestation.
Suddenly she got an idea -
And started shouting " Free free free!"
Everyone gathered around her
She cried - "Save trees, get oxygen free".

MANSI SOLANKI

Mansi Solanki from Navsari, Gujarat. She is currently pursing diploma civil engineering from Uka Tarsadia university. She have started writing a month ago and she loves to write poems, shayari, quotes, one liner. She is CoAuthor of 40+ anthologies and thank you for giving her chance for this anthology.

Instagram id - @inked_solace26

Book Benchers

She still remembered
When first time you looked at her,
She would be writing about you for the rest of her
life.
And you are like drug for her,
You get her high
But nothing lasted forever,
Your fingers were like smoothness of lily stem.
You're in her heart, mind and tongue like souvenir
You admired her like masterpiece and your stupid
conversation means more to her than you think.
When she whisper your name even the moon smiles
and stars shine,
You were a mere stranger who turned out to be her
big smile,
You will reflect in her words, thoughts, stories and
memories like sunlight in the moon,
Her only regret was why she didn't met you earlier.

BIBHUSMITA SINGH SAMANTA

Writer Bibhusmita Singh Samanta writes motivational shayari , quotes , small poems about love , friendship etc .. She believes that , if once you fell in love , then you will start enjoying your life in a different way . Love makes your life complete and joyful . It's a beautiful feeling that can't be explained within words . It can only be felt . So keep loving and spread the positive vibes of love everywhere …

Instagram username - royal_princess_bibhusmita

<u>DEEP INSIDE MY HEART :</u>

Now that you are here ,
I have nothing to fear .
When you is where I belong ,
I knew it , I feel it , so strong .
Nothing has been more clear ,
That it is your love I hold so dear .
Deep inside is the cry of my heart ,
I never ever want us to part .

I'm a hopeless , romantic woman ,
Doing the best I can ,
To show you for sure ,
That my love for you is pure ..
I'll do whatever it takes ,
I don't care about the stakes,
You and only you , I want ,
A prayer I know God will grant ..

ROZY PAUL

Her name is Rozy Paul.She belongs to the tea-estate called Dibrugarh,Assam.She has done M.A. in journalism.Her hobbies are reading,gardening and cooking.She likes travelling a lot.

Instagram id - Writer_rozypaul

<u>CORONA CURSE</u>

People use nature's gift like a waste.They don't use biodegradable garage disposal.People take advantage of nature and it's usage.One day nature takes revenge.A tiny disguise virus killed so many people.This virus makes this heavenly world into hell.People are crying and helpless at its hand.Corona so as curse to human being and all.

SRESTHA RAM

My name is Srestha Ram. Am a student right now and other than studying i engage myself in painting and writing. Am an amateur writer just penning down her thoughts. I love to enjoy happy little moments. Inshort am a girl full of life.

Instagram id - @_.sressss._

Book Benchers

Drops of rain shows your face
I find you in every surface

Those grassy hair on that chubby face
Those memories would always chase

I still remember when you first said sorry
The action depicted that you too worry

I can never forget our first hug
My heart came out with a huge throng

Though we have together our memories few
Still i can live with it coz i love you

-Srestha Ram

POETRY KHAKHOLIA

नमस्कार, ये है पोइट्री खाखोलिया
गुवाहाटी असम से, बीयालिस वर्ष, कॉन्वेंट एजुकेटेड ,
शादीशुदा दो बच्चे है। इन्होंने एमकॉम,
म.इड, एलएलबी किया है पर लिखना इनकी रुचि रही है
स्कूल से ही और अब इसी क्षेत्र में एक मुकाम अर्जित
करना चाहती। इन्होंने चालीस से ज्यादा अंथोलॉजी में
अपनी लेखनी से नवाजा है और कहानी किताब भी लिख
रही है जो जल्द ही आने वाली। लिखना सिर्फ काम नहीं
बल्कि जुनून है इनके लिए जो ये हर पल जीती।
आशा है आप सभी को इनकी रचना पसंद आए।

Instagram id - hidden_desire_06

इश्क़ आस और लाल गुलाब

तेरी मेरी अनछुई सी मोहब्बत
की दास्तां छिपी है इस लाल गुलाब में तू ना आया मौसम
बदल गया फिजाएं बदल गई।
हवा का रुख भी बदल गया
कब सावन बरसा कब गरम हवा का झोंखा आया डाली
से सूखे पत्ते झड़ गए और इसके साथ ही
झड़ गया पतझड़ का मौसम भी।
और आ गई बर्फ सी अगन लगाती सर्दी, सारे मौसम हवा
पानी फिज़ा सब आए और चले भी गए पर तू ना आया।
तेरी यादों का कहर है बरपा
अब तो आजा ना स्ता ना तड़पा
तेरे इंतज़ार में आज भी
लाल गुलाब है खिला रखी।

NILOFAR FAROOQUI TAUSEEF

Meet Nilofar Farooqui Tauseef, born and brought up from Bihar Sharif, Nalanda but living in Mumbai. She has done MCA, MBA and she is Software Engineer in IT. She loves penning down her thoughts, emotions through her writing. For her "Pen is a sword to bring revolution". She wants to make a new changes in life by the motivational quotes or speeches. You can check her fb and instagram handle - @writernilofar

हाल-ए-दिल

कशमकश में है दिल, साज़िश कुछ और है।
ख़्वाहिश कुछ और है, नवाज़िश कुछ और है।

बेबसी का आलम, किस दरख़्त की शाख को बताए?
गुलशन भी खाक हुआ है, क्या हाल , चमन को सुनाए?

परिंदे के मानिंद उड़ कर, काश...आशियाँ चले जाते।
माँ के क़दमों में सर रखकर, सुकून की नींद सो जाते।

पापा की मिट्टी की खुशबू अपने दिल से लगाकर।
अश्क आँखों में भर, चूमते, फिर पेशानी से लगाते।

बड़ा बेचैन हुआ बैठा है दिल, कोई दवा तो बता दो।
दवा गर है नहीं मुमकिन, तो कोई दुआ ही सीखा दो।

सुकून की तलाश में, कब तक भटके हम वीरानों में।
कब तक तलाशते रहे चेहरे, अपनो को बेगानो में।

कफ़स और आह वज़ारी, कभी तो रंग लाएगी।
मायूस न हो, कहता है दिल, दुनिया तेरी बदल जाएगी।
मायूस न हो, कहता है दिल, दुनिया तेरी बदल जाएगी।

MOHANAPRIYA.K

Mohanapriya.K is a budding writer from Tamilnadu, India. She has completed her Bachelor's degree in Engineering stream. She has been a writer for one year as her passion. She wants to be a best compiler and voice over artist in future. She has been co-author of 210 anthologies so far and worked in many record holding, internationally published anthologies and magazines. She participated in many writing contests on instagram and received certificates. Yet she sincerely hope that this writing journey of her will continue as sweetly as it is now and will bring her many successes. You can find her writings on her instagram page.

Instagram : @colours_honey_official

E-mail : doraa.kutty@gmail.com

FACE YOUR BATTLES WITH SMILES

No matter how many difficulties in your life you
should not lose your laughter for it.
Because not laughing means no problem is going to
go right.
But if we handle our problems with a smile and
fight, there is a lot of chance that it will get better.
We do not know when or what will happen in our
life.
The next minute is a life of uncertainty.
So learn to live the life you live in peace and
happiness.
You are the top most priority for you.
Don't lose yourself for anyone.
Anyone can change anyway but the relationship
between you and you will never change.
Just accept yourself.

SMILE IS A STRONGEST WORD

Smile is a huge sword.
It is a weapon that destroys all problems in an
instant.
For that, do not finish the process halfway. Yes, a
good start is a good end - they say.
But everything that happens in this world depends
on our hard work and effort.
So the beginning can be anyway, but we hope its
end will be a good one.
Because that decision depends on the time too.
Love, caring, Warmth, affection get used to living
with these love to love avoid being hatred.
Never be afraid of retribution, sarcasm etc.
Do not be afraid to stop your trips to victory.
Because you know they are not true.
Motivate Yourself!

- Mohanapriya.K

Book Benchers

ANKITA NAHAR

#AKII#@@@ अंकिता नाहर मूल रूप से अजमेर, राजस्थान की रहने वाली हैं। ये लिखने के लिए हमेशा उत्साहित रहती है साथ ही हमेशा शब्दों से सुकून सा पाती हैं। ये अपने विचारों और जो भी इन्होंने अपनी जिंदगी से सीखा है, अनुभव लिया है उसे अपनी रचनाओं में लिख देती हैं। इससे इनकी रचनाएँ बहुत ही ज्यादा भावुक भावों वाली और प्रभावशाली बन जाती हैं। जो कि पढ़ने वालों को बहुत आकर्षित करती है। वह इस माध्यम को और आगे तक ले जाना चाहती हैं। आप इनकी रचनाओं को इंस्टाग्राम @naharankita1 पर पढ़ सकते हैं।

एक समय था जब एक दूजे के पास
इतनी बातें थीं करने को,
अब तो मात्र चुप्पियां ही हैं
जो ये रिश्ता निभा रही हैं।

वो सिर्फ मेरा दीदार करने के वास्ते
ना जाने कितने तिकड़म लगता था,
और एक जल्ली से मैं
बचपन की नादानियां समझ के छोड़ आये।

मैं तेरा इंतजार उम्र भर कर लूं
पर तुम इतना तो कह दो एक बार,
की मैं किसी और का कैसे हो सकता हूं
मैं तो सिर्फ तुम्हारा हूं ।

Book Benchers

GOURI VISHWANATH SALVI

A girl with a human heart , pursuing TYBAF, have
high goals of serving the needy, A happy heart ,
interested in accounts, upcoming famous writer,
Still have a skill in designing and arts and also
wrote in various anthologies

Instagram id - @gouri.salvi

<u>DEEP THOUGHT</u>

A story of teen age girl where i found my first love.
A bollywood type love story was happily going but
one day the devil of her life got the information that
she is happy and smiling from the bottom of her
heart ... She wrote her a letter of friendship which
gave her the hope that she can have a real big sister
instead of a devil but that was a trap set to know her
secrets. Her secrets were revealed she fell in that
trap! A heart was torned , eyes were swollen her life
was about to be broken but her lover formed a trap
for her sister they spread the rumours about their
breakup but they were still happy together but who
knew that those lies spread will become true...

Moral :- Trust none, but don't break your human self

<u>QUOTES</u>

" Trust none,
Let your humanity shine"

"It's not the matter of heart,
It's the matter of living quality"

"Love in your heart is enough for you in your life,
You don't need anyone, you just need your heart of
love"

"A heart guides, A mind believes,
A soul thrives, Adrenaline rushes"

SUMANDRITA PAUL

Annyeonghaseyo.
She is Sumandrita paul.
Her nickname is Hiya.
Her age is 13 years.
She is being 6 times co-author of the 6 books till now.
She stays in West Bengal Durgapur.
She is a very good dancer,artist and singer and loves to write books which would be thrilling for people who are reading.
Her aim is to become air hostess,kpop idol or modeler.
She is a girl of fulfilling her dreams to have a bright future ahead.

Instagram id - GURLL.WITH.LUV

<u>WE PURPLE U BTS</u>

The 7 stars of the Seoul
To whom we are the only
Armies and though.....
There loves and emotions
Inspires us.....
Where as they are ready to give
There heart's as well as there
Life too for us........

There presentation and outfits
Heals our heart,
There dances and songs
Which make us feel;
There love for us.
We purple u 7 jewel's....
As armies are always
in ur heart....

No matter what happens...
Armies r there for u all,
As u all are the shining
Stars or in other words
the 7 heroes of the Seoul.....

PRIYA DAS

She is Priya Das an amazing writer from a beautiful land of Northeast India. Coauthor of more than 80+ anthologies. A trained artist, blogger, calligrapher and a author of 18 years old.

Instagram id - @the_poet_gallery

From classmates to best friends.
From notes sharing to caring.
A rose of love began to blossom in my heart
for him.
But over time his thorns started torment me,
when I came to know about his beloved.
The beautiful rose of my love withered and
shattered into broken pieces of my tears.
Friendship which turned into one sided love
ended forever but even today I am paying
the price for the crime which I have
committed to love someone unconditionally.

<u>RAVISHANKER NISHAD (ARVI)</u>

Co-author Ravishanker Nishad (ARVI) is good
writer from Raigarh (Chhattisgarh).
he has completed his in science stream .
he has been writing poetry for 2 years as his passion
. He has to writeup many anthology and he is good
to be a part of the society . he is inspired by many
famous and very best writer poets like Mahakavi
Kalidas, Sumitranandan Pant , maithili sharan gupt ,
mahakavi Ramdhari sinh dinkar , he also favorite
now present day kumar vishwas and Rahat indauri
sahab ,
he want to be favorite and famous writer in future

...

Instagram username - @arvinishad

दिलों पर ख्यालों की बर्फ जमीं है
भीगा सा है आलम निगाहों में नमी है ।
सब ज़ख्म गहरे से हैं
लम्हात सभी ठहरे से हैं ।।
झूमकर पर्वत पर घटा छा रही है ।
प्यार की लगन करीब आ रही है ।।
खुली है आंखें मगर
निगाहों में पर्दा सा छाया है ।
दिल के हालात नाज़ुक से हैं
मन बहुत घबराया सा है ।।
अंजामों की सोच कहानी
मन में तूफ़ान समाया सा है ।।
बेचैनी है तुझे पाने की
चाहत पर अपने मर मिट जाने की ।

राह ये मोहब्बत की आसान नहीं है
दिलों का मामला है कोई सामान नहीं है ।।
गुजरता वक्त भी थम जाएगा
आंसू भी बारिश बनकर बरस जाएगा ।।
वादे इरादे सारे झूठे से लगते हैं
जरूरत आती है जब उम्मीदें टूटने से लगते हैं ।
दिल तो बेचारा है
कभी हंसता है कभी रोता है ।।
मंजिलें किसी को मिलती है
कोई इसके लिए सब कुछ खोता है ।।
जिंदगी का ये खेल है
कहीं बिछड़ना है कहीं मेल है ।।
कहीं सूखा है रेगिस्तान रेत का
कहीं समुंदर में अगाध पानी है ।।
हंसना रोना लगा रहता है
यही ज़िंदगी की कहानी है ।।

<u>SANA SHAIKH</u>

Sana is post graduate who likes to share her experience and can go to any extend to make people smile.
She prefers to help people and keep everyone guessing how come she be so cool.
A friendly and a lovely heart for enhancing a better relationship with people around her.
She prefers to speak whatever she notices be a dream or a reality which sometimes people try to hide.
Sometimes she used to be a silent girl but now she's one who can speak against anything and can go to any extend to fulfill her dream (A writer)

Instagram id - khidkikeuspaar

FEELING - A STORY OF A SHY GIRL

My name is Sana and I'm not a terrorist
Jokes apart
I was a very shy girl and hardly I made 5 to 6 friends in my entire school life. Sounds odd but that's truth. Everyone used to make fun of me by calling "Chana" "Chana" and I wouldn't reiterate back and that became their plus point. I wasn't popular as my sisters were. Then came the turning point when I joined my Junior College. There I made a lot of friends and my helping nature helped in developing friendship. One of my friend advised me if you can reiterate just give a smile back. A shy girl too has a feeling and doesn't wants to be someone's pet or be in limelight. Even a shy girl can talk but needs someone to encourage her. So please guys don't take advantage of anyone Qki sabka time aayega. There the sayings go "tit for tat" Mind you if a shy girl opens her mouth you'll be left with no words to say

Khali ko jaise phool bane waqt lagta hai
Waise hi ek shaant ladki ko chulbuli bane waqt lagta hai

So sorry I kept this story up to Junior College but
my graduation and post-graduation friends too
encouraged me.
Love you all friends and thanks for always being
my support.

<u>KOVIDHA</u>

Kovidha hails from Hyderabad, Telangana.. She like to decorate her words and emotions on paper and has participated in various anthologies..Additionally,
She wants to be unique! to stand out amongst the people and like to learn new things. She believes in delivering smiles on the faces. u can find her writings in IG as evil_dweller585

<u>SOUL</u>

Though the sun sets and finalizes another day,
It leaves us with an array of color and hope,
Hope that a new day will come,
Hope that life with you will continue to be as
beautiful
As it is now.
It fills my heart with gladness knowing that
Though the sun is being replaced with night,
When I lay my head to rest,
You will be by my side,
Comforting me tonight.

S. T. RENUKA THANGAVEL

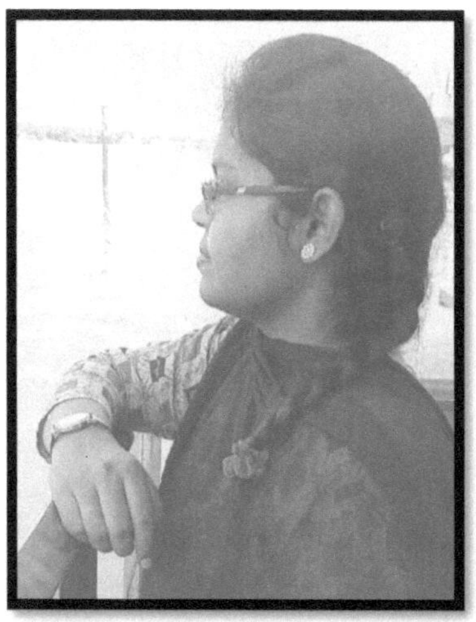

S. T. Renuka Thangavel from Thirunelveli, She is currently pursuing her BE degree in Government College of Engineering. She has great interest in writing ; exploring her Motherland INDIA and beautiful Nature.

Instagram id - @thamizhvaan

<u>HOLD ON</u>

Hold on to your
Self confidence -
so that nothing can
shake you...

Hold on to your Goal
so that no divergence can
Interfere you...

Hold on to your Enthusiasm
so that no feebleness can
hinder you...

Hold on strong to
your Magnificent Soul
so that you can move on
towards your Eternal
Glorious and happy life !

<u>MY DEAR MOON...</u>

Like a cute little child
peeping behind his
Beloved Mother -
You show your bright face
either whole or hiding it partial
in our beautiful Mother
Earth's massive shadow ! -
However you arrive and appear
I'm getting filled with Pleasure ;
Excitement and blissful Happiness
Whenever I see you !
My Dear Moon...

N.KRISHNAVENI

N. Krishnaveni is an aspiring writer and a budding poet. One of her poems "My Beloved Damsel!" has published in The Literary Herald journal. She is a co-author of many anthologies. She won the Spectrum Budding Writer Award 2021. Most of her poems deals with the theme of nature, human emotions, and philosophical thoughts. Her poetry voices out the deepest emotions and secrets that are left unspoken and destined to be beautifully inked. Having a creative artistic propaganda, her writings hails from the articulate thoughts with coherence, spontaneity and flowery language.

Instagram username - krishi_aju

<u>WHY IT HAPPENS?</u>

Thoughts in the head loosely hung
Like the strings in the wind chimes.
Plays the music that lures everyone
Dragging the senses to the fruitful measures.
In the world of masked faces,
Everyone dealt with their own fears
Happily hides them all behind the walls.
We would not have lost you
If the world had changed its perception
And accepted you the way you are.
But at times things won't happen like the way we
wish
Rather, it will be, "why it happens like this?"

DEESHA SONI

Deesha Soni..a Post Graduate and M.phil adorns the hat of a
multitasker of an educationist,artist,poet,photographer,author ,
blogger,homemaker,wife and mother...
She has 10 years experience in the field of Education as a
Professor and Coordinator.Deesha has various publications to
her credit in national and international levels.
Deesha has various published works to her credit... she has
two books published on Amazon... named 'Just thoughts' and
'Random thoughts on pandemic'..Kindle edition and more than
100 plus published works on various online platforms of ..
Deesha has been twice nominated for Author of a week award
by Storymirror and has also won various recognitions in
penning stories and write-ups.. at National and International
levels...
Deesha has various published works to her credit... she has
two books published on Amazon... named 'Just thoughts' and
'Random thoughts on pandemic'..Kindle edition has also won
many prizes in National and international levels in many
write-ups...
Deesha has also published her works in 300 plus anthologies
of multiple genres..
Instagram id - Deeshagauree

Corruption....
Corruption in soul...and deeds...
Greed and Selfish are corruption seeds...
Sanity of senses blow up in the air....
Under corrupt deeds... everything is fair...
Sold off are ethics and principles...in the market of
corruption...
Mean and Conspiracy is selling high in auction...
Rationality and fairness are crushed below feet...
Evil workshops are active... when corrupts meet...
Shame has no existence... shameless is at win...
All the justful acts go into trash bin...
Corruption is a way to flourish and prosper for
some..
But forget do they... that their end is near to come....
Scared aren't they to perform cheating business...
Loot and Rob they...to innocent by faulty means...
The corrupt thinks they're always right...
And crush the one's against them who fight...
Corruption is an ancient practice...
Right from Ramayan to Mahabharat...it hasn't gone
amiss....
Corruption is a vicious trap. ..
The righteous are treated like crap....
But don't forget good has always conquered evil....
The angels of honesty have killed the corrupt
devil....

V.S.KAARTHIKVEL

A budding writer who loves to play with words
interested in story writing, poetry and lyric writing.
He had worked as co author in few anthologies and
written two album songs in Tamil and publishing
his quotes through his blog in Instagram

Instagram id - kavi_pithan05

LIFE IS A PAINTING

Life is like doing a painting
There will be a general format or theory to paint a
beautiful painting
Everyone would be following the same strokes and
patterns
But only the painting which has its own uniqueness
will be more beautiful
So,Make your painting with your style
Lead your life by creating and following your own
style

COWARDS CANNOT SUCEED ?

Every human in this world would have been a
coward at sometimes
He becomes brave when he starting believing
himself
Self belief is the only key to unlock your fear in
your life
A human who fails to unlock his fear is being
termed as coward

<u>HEALTH IS WEALTH</u>

Physical and mental health are the basic two bricks
in which a big building named life have been built
Maintain those bricks properly otherwise the life
becomes collapsed

SHRIYA SINGH

Shriya Singh is an Indian writer who writes really deep and beautiful poetries . Her writings have been published in several big magazines and newspapers. She's a co-author of a number of anthologies and also the founder of ' Letterishh ' which is a very well known name in the writing world . She is a really hardworking individual in every field and is currently working on her upcoming debut book.

Instagram id - @letterishh

Book Benchers

That gaze was a sin
and your eyes a sinner
for like a ray emitted
intent to make mine go blind
yet my unhinged self
wanting to look back again
knowing it would turn me to ashes
But something inside my chest
whispered that the phoenix of love
is born here in pain
it has to walk down the stones
it has to die to get to thrones
and in that moment
my heart beat again
Astonished at how a gaze
could make me die & be born AGAIN..

UNNATI SAWANT

She is a budding and bubbly writer expressing her creative mind in pen and ink. Born in city of dreams , passionate to travel round the world . Aspires to become CA.

Book Benchers

To get inside edge of my heart ;
You have to be smart .
Life is so unpredictable ;
Be capable .

Immature and pure soul ;
Burning like a coal .
Dreams seem to be bubble ;
Works is full trouble .

Never giving is key ;
To the lock of my heart .
Journey may be painful ;
But end result maybe colourful .

To get inside edge of my heart;
You have to be smart .

NAZRANA AHSAN WANI

She's Nazrana Ahsan wani Daughter of Mohammad
Ahsan wani.
She's 17 years old Girl and she was Born in
Paradise, where The snow cladded mountains, the
blooming fresh buds, the golden meadows add to
the mesmerizing beauty of nature.
Her birthplace is in the beautiful District by the
name Bandipora,which is surrounded by rivulets,
brooks, and mountains on the banks of Wullar Lake.
She's pursuing her studies in class 12th.

Instagram id - Mystify_anu16.

<u>A DREAM KILLER</u>

My words can't describe how much I hate you,
The day you entered my life it was all ruined,
The happiness was temporary,
But the pain was permanent,
With your hateful plans,
You took everything from me,
Now I have nothing left but the hatred,
For you in my heart beneath,
I will not let you ruin my future,
I will not believe your silly convincing words,
Now my life is just what I need it to be,
I will do right by my side,
You left me to rot when I was sad,
And now I have convinced my heart,
That I will fight until I break you apart.

~Wani Anu.

<u>PRAGATI GIRI</u>

Pragati Giri lives in UP state, district Varanasi.She is graduated in life sciences and now she's an Passionate Writer, Compiler of 15-16 anthologies, co-author of 60+ anthologies and Project Head I'm three Publication in writing industry.

Instagram id - @writerpragati5409

<u>INNER HEART :</u>

A inner heart wanted to talk to myself
With his both veins and both arteries
And they told me always be yours
But be to go with pure blood
Does not matter how many
Bacterias & foreign particles
Are there in your blood.
If your heart will be pure
With very sure enzymes which
Helps you to boost up of your fitness
And health
Only who,can imagine something you
With the better understanding
And comes in lining to increase
Your level by outer epidermal layer
Of body & your physical health.

Pragati Giri

SRIJITA SAHA

Co-author Srijita Saha is a good writer from Kolkata.She has completed her.education in 12th in science stream. She has been writing poetry for 2-3 months as her passion. She wants to be a writer in future.

Instagram id - feel_words_of_quoetry

<u>MY HEART</u>

My heart silently beats for you,
Chose the special you among all other crew.
My heart is half of you,
Let no pain be in due,
My heart prays for your safety,
Your mind is more prettier than the outer beauty.
My heart is yours,
No one can break our bond with any outward force.
My heart is healed,
When my life gets with you filled.